Post-Revolutionary

Cuban Spanish:

A Glossary of Social, Political, and Common Terms

(Spanish - English)

Glosario de términos socio-políticos y

autóctonos de actualidad

(Español-Inglés)

Post-Revolutionary

Cuban Spanish:

A Glossary of Social, Political, and Common Terms

(Spanish - English)

Glosario de términos socio-políticos y

autóctonos de actualidad

(Español-Inglés)

by

Jesús Núñez Romay

blue ocean press
tokyo

Published by:

blue ocean press, an Imprint of Aoishima Research Institute (ARI)
#807-36 Lions Plaza Ebisu
3-25-3 Higashi, Shibuya-ku
Tokyo, Japan 150-0011

mail@aoishima-research.com
URL: http://www.blueoceanpublishing.com
        http://www.aoishima-research.com

Cover Design by romeo carlos

ISBN: 978-4-902837-06-4

In loving memory of my parents

PROLOGUE

The first edition of this glossary subsequently enlarged and now in its fourth printing triggered considerable interest, clearly demonstrating its usefulness.

The product of patient research that its young, enthusiastic, and tireless author carried out over the course of five years in the little free time left him from his teaching duties, this glossary unquestionably fills a lexicographic vacuum that had long existed in Cuba.

The determining factor in the development of languages now, as in its origins is the social praxis of men and women. Thus, as a social instrument par excellence, a language and especially the lexical aspect of it always reflects the changes that occur in society.

Because the first socialist revolution in the Americas took place in Cuba, this country has also seen the rise of new terms and the introduction of new, very specific meanings for old terms, adopted as required to express new realities. How can these neologisms be rendered in English, when no English-speaking country has as yet carried out a Marxist-Leninist social revolution and, therefore, no ready-made equivalents are available? This situation has been a poser not only for translators but also for language teachers and other professionals whose work required frequent contact with English.

The present glossary should be exceptionally useful to all of them.

Obviously, a glossary including terms from all spheres of human activity would require many years of work. The author has thus limited himself to collecting the terms most often used in the sociopolitical sphere of daily life, and in this field, he has produced a wealth of up-to-date material.

Marjorie Moore Reynolds, Ph.D.

Full Professor,

Instituto Superior de Ciencias Médicas de La Habana

Author´s note

A revolution triumphed in Cuba in 1959, making it the first socialist country in the Americas.

The Cuban Revolution sprang from the need to make thoroughgoing political and economic transformations - which, in turn, created a need for new terms to express them.

Cuba's growing international prestige and new diplomatic, trade and cultural relations led us to look for new equivalents in foreign languages so we could communicate with the rest of the world.

The problem of how to describe in foreign languages concepts and things that do not exist in the countries in which those languages are spoken is extremely challenging.

In tackling this problem, and to reduce bias and arbitrariness, we compared texts from the Granma Weekly Review and Tricontinental, Prisma, Soberania and Cuba Internacional magazines. We then consulted five translators and a professor with more than twenty-five years of experience in this field in order to reach a consensus on the terms included in this glossary and their equivalents.

This has been the result of our painstaking work.

Cuban terms not related to work   (a)

Sociopolitical terms   (b)

Terms related to different aspects of work   (c)

Notice that the dialectical interrelationship linking the various spheres of the activities carried out by a single individual leads to the frequent overlapping of classifications.

Each term is listed in the section where it is most used.

Some terms,however,may appear in two or three classifications.

Glossary

(Spanish - English)

Glosario

(Español-Inglés)

A

abanderado: standard bearer (a,b)

abanderamiento: presentation of a flag (b)

abatizar: water treatment (a)

abonar (una asignatura): an exemption (c)

acantonado: (dícese de las tropas) quartered, billeted (c)

acción sostenida: (en medicamentos) sustained release (a,c)

acomodamiento: (actitud negativa) sponging, job complacency (a)

acopio: (centros) state collection (center, enterprise, agency) (c)

activismo: animation (b)

activista: activist (a,b)

activo de vigilancia: vigilance meeting (c)

acto: Rally (a)

    cultural: entertainment program (a)

    central: main ceremony (b)

    político-cultural: political-cultural program (b)

    deportivo-cultural: sports-entertainment program (a)

    de reafirmación revolucionaria: revolutionary reaffirmation meeting (b)

acuartelado: (en lo militar) quartered, billeted (b)

adiestramiento: Hands-on-training, on-the-job training (c)

administrador: manager (b)

adoctrinamiento: indoctrination (b)

afectaciones en los servicios: interruptions (b)

    en un desastre natural: adverse effects (b)

afiliado: (a una organización) member;dues-paying member (b,c)

agregado cultural: cultural attaché (c)

agricultura colectivizada: collectivized agriculture (c)

agromercado: market for fresh meat and produce (a)

agrupación campesina: farm grouping (c)

> **ganadera**: livestock farm grouping (c)

> **genética**: breeders group (c)

aguardiente: high wine (a)

aguerrido: seasoned, veteran (b,c)

alarma aérea: air-raid alarm (b)

alarma de combate: call to arms (b)

a la ofensiva: on the offensive (b,c)

albergue de estudiantes o trabajadores: dorm, dormitory (c)

> **de personas desamparadas**: shelter (a)

alfabetizador: literacy teacher (a)

alevines: (centro de) fish spawn center (c)

alianza obrero-campesina: worker-farmer alliance (c)

alto rendimiento: (in sports) high yield, (in athletes) high performance

alumnos ayudantes: student assistant, student-aide, student teacher (c)

alumno insertado: student helper (c)

alzados en Cuba (antes del triunfo de la Revolución): rebels (b)

> (en general): insurgents (b)

ambientación: interior decorating (a)

ámbito: environment, sphere (a)

alzadoras (de caña): cane loaders (c)

anillo lechero: dairy belt (c)

amonestación: warning, admonition, reprimand (c)

animales afectivos: pets (a)

ante-proyecto: draft,preliminary draft (b)

antigüedad (años de servicio en el trabajo): seniority (c)

antisocial: anti-social (b)

apadrinamiento: sponsoring (a)

apagón: blackout, power outage (a)

aparato estatal: state machinery (b)

aparceros: share croppers (c)

apátrida (en general): stateless (b)

(si abandona el país): expatriate (b)

(si es expulsado): exile, outcast (b)

a pie de obra: work on job site (c)

aprovechamiento de la norma potencial de molida: operating at full capacity (c)

apuntalar: (una casa) to prop up a house with scaffolding (a), to shore up a house (a)

arbitraje estatal: state arbitration (c)

arcas del estado: coffers, treasury of the state (b)

área de atención: local military office (b,c)

áreas verdes: parks, lawns, landscaping (a)

armamentismo: arms build up, military build up (b)

arribista: climber, johnny came lately (b)

arroz precocido: parboiled rice (c)

artes manuales: manual training, shop (a)

artes plásticas: visual arts (a)

artistas aficionados: amateur entertainers (a)

Asalto al Cuartel Moncada: Attack on the Moncada Garrison (b)

asaltantes: participants in the attack (b)

asamblea de balance: assembly of review (b)

    de ejemplares: assembly of exemplary workers or students (b)

    municipal del Poder Popular: municipal assembly of people's power (b)

    de rendición de cuentas: assembly for rendering accounts (b)

    de representantes: assembly of union representatives (b)

    de renovación y/o ratificación de mandatos: assembly for the renewal and/or ratification of mandates (b)

    de méritos y deméritos: assembly of merits and demerits (b)

aseguramiento de la calidad: guaranteeing quality (c)

asesor: adviser (c)

asignación: (de equipos o materiales) allocation (c)

asilo de ancianos: home for the aged, home for the elderly (a)

    político: political asylum (b)

asistencia (espiritual): a glass of water for the spirit. (a).

    (si es comida): offering (a)

asistente: (de círculos infantiles) attendants (c)

asociación nacional de innovadores y racionalizadores: national association of innovators and rationalizers (c)

asociación nacional de agricultores pequeños: national association of small farmers (c)

asociación nacional de ciegos y débiles visuales: national association of blind and visually impaired (a)

aspirantes al partido: party candidates (b)

ataque sorpresivo: blitz attack (b)

atención al hombre: direct concern to the needs and interests of the individual (a,c)

atención integral: comprehensive medical care (c)

atención primaria: primary health care (c)

atentado: assassination attempt (b)

atributos nacionales: national tree, national flower, national bird

royal palm tree, butterfly lily, Cuban trogon

atributos pioneriles: Pioneer's neckerchief and badge (c)

ausentismo: absenteeism (c)

ausentista: absentee (c)

austeridad revolucionaria: revolutionary austerity (b)

autenticación: legalization (c)
autoconsumo: consumption in the province; home consumption; self-supply (a)

autopista: expressway; freeway (a,c)

autoservicio: K.P. (kitchen police) (a,c)

autosustentabilidad: self –sustainability (a,c)

autor intelectual: (con una connotación positiva) intellect behind, guiding spirit behind, moving spirit behind (b)

(con una connotación negativa) mastermind (b)

auxiliares técnicos: technical assistants (c)

aval: endorsement, indorsement, recommendation (b,c)

avances: (en un campo determinado) gains (a,c)

avanzada: avant garde (c)

avicultor: poultry farmer (c)

ayuda humanitaria: humanitarian assistance,humanitarian aid (a,b)

azúcar a granel: bulk sugar (c)

B

baja (escolar): school dropout

(de un equipo): to write it off,to take it out of promotion (c)

(natural) (de una organización ,por vencerse el tiempo): to automatically lose membership (b)

bajareque: aboriginal Cuban dwelling (a)

balsero: raftsman, boatman (b)

baluarte: bulwark

banco de sangre: blood bank (a,c)

banda del Estado Mayor: General Staff band (a,b)

bandazo: abrupt shift (b)

bandera de lucha: banner of struggle (b)

banderola: streamer, pennant, pennon (a,b)

barbacoa: kind of loft (a)

barbecho: fallow (land) (c)

barreras arquitectónicas: architectural barriers (a)

base de aseguramiento: supply depot

de campismo: camp site; camping area, camping grounds (a)

de cohetes: launching pad (b)

de transporte: parking lot, terminal (c)

de taxis: taxi stand (c)

material: materials, basics (a,c)

bastión inexpugnable: impregnable bastion, impregnable bulwark (b)

Batalla de Ideas: Battle of Ideas (b)

batalla ideológica: ideological struggle (b)

batalla por el noveno grado: battle for the ninth grade (b,c)

batallón de avanzada: avant garde batallion (b)

batey: mill town, mill hamlet, sugar mill community (a)

beca: scholarship, fellowship (c)

becado: boarding student, scholarship student (c)

belicista (política): warmongering policy (b)

biblioteca circulante: circulating library,book mobile library (a,c)

bienes malversados: ill-gotten gains

bienestar: (estado de salud) well-being (a)

      social: social welfare (b)

biofábrica: biofactory (c)

biopreparados: bioproducts

bisutería: costume jewelry (a)

blandenguería: permisiveness, wishy-washyness, spinelessness (b,c)

bloque de la FMC: FMC chapter (a)

      militar: military alliance (b)

bloqueo económico: economic blockade (b)

bohío: palm thatch hut, thatch roofed hut (a)

bolera (sala de juego): bowling alley (a)

bolsa de profesionales: pool of professionals (c)

      de valores: stock market, stock exchange (b)

      negra: black market (b)

bombo (sorteo de visas): visa raffle (b)

bonos de ahorro: saving bonds (a)

      para comprar ropas: coupons (a)

botella (plaza fantasma) sinecure (b)

botellero (persona que pide aventón en la carretera): hitcher (a)

brazalete (identificación para el CDR u otra organización): armband (b)

brazo armado: armed wing, strong arm, armed division (b)

Brigada Especial: task force (b)

brigada fronteriza: border brigade (b)

Brigadas Técnicas Juveniles: Technical Youth Brigades (b,c)

brigadista (de alfabetización): literacy teacher (b)

brote (epidémico): outbreak (a)

bufete colectivo: People's legal counselling bureau (c)

buque-escuela: training ship (c)

buró ejecutivo de la CTC: executive bureau of the central organization of Cuban trade unions (b)

   de dirección: leadership bureau (b)

   político: political bureau (b)

   de orientación de la moda: fashion bureau (c)

   provincial del partido: party provincial bureau (b)

burocratismo: red tape, bureaucracy (b)

C

caballerosidad: gentlemanly behaviour (a,b,c)

Caballero de París: The Gentleman from Paris (a)

cabaña (de playa): cabana (a)

cabecera de municipio: municipality seat (a)

cabecilla: ringleader (b)

cabeza de familia: single parent, head of household (a)

cabeza de playa: beachhead (b)

cabildo: lodge (a)

cacharrear: (en un carro o equipo) to fiddle (a,c)

CADECA: money exchange office (a,c)

cadena puerto-transporte-economía interna: dock-to consumer-distribution chain, off-loading-transportation-distribution network (c)

caja chica: petty cash (c)

cálculo económico: cost-profit accounting (c)

caldo de cultivo: breeding ground (a)

calendario de zafra: harvest time-table (c)

calificadores (para una plaza laboral): requisites, pre-requisites, job description (c)

camaradería: comradery (b,c)

camello: (transporte) truck bus (a)

campamento de pioneros: pioneers' camp (b)

camión pipa: water truck (a)

campaña de alfabetización: literacy campaign (a,b,c)

    de ahorro: savings campaign

    de embellecimiento: sprucing-up campaign

emulativa: emulation campaign

de seguimiento: follow-up campaign

de solidaridad: solidarity campaign

de vacunación: vaccination campaign, vaccination drive

campismo popular: people's camping (c)

campo (bloque): socialist or capitalist camp (b)

campo de tiro a la intemperie: firing range, shooting range (a)

techado: shooting gallery

canasta familiar: food basket (a)

cantera (de la UJC o PCC): pool, reserve, source of potential members

cantos de sirena: siren songs (b)

cañonazo de las nueve: 9 o'clock cannon shot (a,c)

capacitación: training (c)

capacitador: person in charge of advanced training (b)

captación para el Partido: party co-option campaign (b)

en general: recruitment campaign (c)

de divisas: to bring in hard currency (a,b,c)

Caravana de la Amistad: Friendshipment (b)

Caravana de la Libertad: Caravan of Freedom (b)

Caravana Pioneril de la Victoria: Pioneer's Victory Motorcade (b)

cargo (responsabilidad): post (c)

de dirección: executive position (b,c)

carnet de identidad: identity card (a,b,c)

carnet de salud: health certificate (c)

carrera armamentista: arms race (b)

carrera de orientación: orienteering (a,c)

carrera universitaria: major (a,c)

cartelera (de cine): movie section, entertainment section, listings, movie guide (a)

cartilla (de alfabetización): teaching manual (b)

casa de la Cultura: Community Arts Center, Community Cultural Center (c)

casa de tránsito: half-way house

>**consultorio del médico de la familia**: community doctor
>
>home office (a,c)
>
>**de campaña**: field tent (a)
>
>**de descanso**: R and R (rest and relaxation) (a)
>
>**de socorro**: first-aid station (c)
>
>**del joven creador**: House of Young Artists (b)
>
>**del té**: the tea house (a)
>
>**comisionista**: second-hand store (a)
>
>**de bajo consumo**: low cost house (a,c)

casco histórico de La Habana: Colonial Havana (a,b,c)

casilla (de productos industriales): box, square (a)

Castillo de la Real Fuerza: Real Fuerza Castle (a,c)

Castillo de La Punta: La Punta Fortress (a,c)

catre: (cama de lona y madera): cot, field bed (a)

caudillismo: bossism (b)

cederista: CDR member (b)

censo de reserva laboral: labor reserve census (c)

>**de población y vivienda**: housing and population census
>
>(a)

22

central azucarero: sugar mill (c)

centro asistencial: health care center (c)

Centro Nacional de Envases y Embalajes: National Container and Packaging Center (c)

Central de Trabajadores de Cuba: Confederation of Cuban Workers, Central Organization of Cuban Trade Unions (b)

centralismo democrático: democratic centralism (b)

certificado de trabajo comunista: communist labor certificate (b,c)

cerveza dispensada: draft beer

cifras directivas: target figures, programmed figures (c)

cimarrón: run-away slave (a)

cinturón lechero de la Habana: Havana's dairy belt (c)

circular: (información que se hace conocer por escrito en un ámbito determinado): circular, announcement (c)

círculo de estudio: study group

   de interés: science club, vocational study group

   infantil: day-care center

   social obrero: workers' social club

   de abuelos: senior citizens club (a,b)

circuito de estreno: first-run movies (a)

circunscripción: circumscription, constituency, electoral district, precinct (a,b)

citación (legal): summons (c)

ciudad escolar: school city (a,c)

claustro (de profesores): teaching staff, faculty (c)

climatización: air conditioning, refrigeration (a,c)

código de familia: family code (a,b,c)

código del trabajo: labor code (c)

coexistencia pacífica: peaceful coexistence (b)

colarse (en un lugar): to butt in, to jump the queue (a,c)

colegios electorales: polling places (b)

coleros: queue hustlers, queue sharks (a,c)

Columna Juvenil del Centenario: Centennial Youth Column (c)

Columna Juvenil del Trabajo: Working Youth Detachment (c)

comandancia general: general headquarters (b,c)

Comandante en Jefe Fidel Castro: Commander in Chief Fidel Castro (b)

combatiente: fighter, combatant, trooper (b)

> **de Girón**: Girón veteran (b)

> **internacionalista**: internationalist fighter (b)

combinado agrícola: poultry complex (c)

comedor obrero: workers' dining halls (c)

comisión permanente: standing committee (b,c)

> **de agitación y propaganda**: agit - prop commission (b)

> **de glosas**: auditing commission (c)

comité de base (UJC): grass-roots committee (b)

> **de dirección**: executive committee (c)

> **de defensa de la revolución**: Committee for the Defense of the Revolution (a,b)

> **militar**: conscription office (b)

> **estatal del trabajo y seguridad social**: state committee for labor and social security (c)

> **estatal de finanzas**: state committee for finance (c)

> **provincial del PCC**: provincial party committee (b)

de protección física: work safety committee, security committee (c)

de redaccción: drafting committee (c)

de zona: zone committee (b)

comprometido (partidario consecuente con una causa o idea): a committed person (b)

compromisos laborales: work pledges, work commitments, production targets (c)

compañero: comrade, colleague (b,c)

compañía motorizada: motorized company (c)

comparsa: carnival troupe, street dance groups (a)

comunicado conjunto: joint communique (b)

Comunidad de Estados Independientes: Community of Independent States (a,b)

concentración de masas: mass rally (a,b,c)

concentrado (curso intensivo que se recibe en un corto período de tiempo): crash course (b,c)

conciencia política: political awareness (b)

condecorar: decorate (a)

condición Listos para la Defensa: Ready-for-Defense status (b)

Conferencias Cumbres: Summit Conferences (b)

conformismo (actitud negativa): complacency (a,b)

confronta (horario) off peak bus,off peak service (a,c)

congelar un trámite: to paralyze a transaction

un salario: to freeze a wage

una zona: to seal a zone (a,c)

Conjunto Nacional de Espectáculos: National Variety Ensemble (a)

consagración (al trabajo, a la defensa, al estudio): dedication (b,c)

consecuente (con principios): consistent with, staunch supporter (b)

Consejo de Ayuda Mutua Económica: Council for Mutual Economic Assistance (b)

>   **de dirección**: administration board, directory board, board of directors (c)

>   **de estado**: council of state (b)

>   **de escuela**: school council (a,c)

>   **de defensa**: defense council (a,b,c)

>   **de familia**: family council (a)

>   **de guerra**: court martial (b)

>   **de ministros**: council of ministers (b)

>   **de padres y maestros**: parent-teacher association (PTA) (a)

>   **de trabajo**: work council (c)

>   **de seguridad**: security council (b)

>   **de vecinos**: neighbors council (a)

>   **populares**: people's council (a)

consigna revolucionaria: revolutionary slogan (b)

conquistas del pueblo: People's achievements, gains (b)

Consignatarias Mambisas: Mambisas Ship Chandlers Enterprise (c)

Consolidados (talleres): repair shops

consultorio vivienda: Home office

contenido de trabajo: job description, task description (c)

contingente: contingent (b,c)

contrata: part-time job, contract (c)

contravenciones: misdemeanors (a)

control y ayuda: control and assistance inspection, supervision, check up (c)

coordinador de los CDR: CDR coordinator (b)

cooperativa: cooperative (c)

convalidar (una asignatura): to accept the credit for (a subject) (a)

convención turística: travel trade show (a)

convocatoria para una reunión: to call a meeting (b)

       a un concurso o certamen: announcement of a contest

       (c)

convoyar: (un producto con otro): to sell in tandem with (a,c)

Cordón de La Habana: Havana green belt (c)

correlación de fuerzas: balance of forces (b)

corresponsalía: correspondent's office (c)

cortinas rompevientos: windbreaks, wind barriers (c)

cotizar: to pay dues; to collect dues (a,c)

crecimiento (UJC o PCC): growth (b)

crítica constructiva: constructive criticism (b,c)

Crisis de Octubre: October Missile Crisis (b)

cronograma: flowchart (a)

cuadro (laboral o político): cadre (b,c)

       (de honor) honor roll (b,c)

Cuartel Moncada: Moncada Garrison (b)

cubículo: cubbyhole (a)

cuentapropista: freelance, self -employed worker (c)

cuerpo diplomático: diplomatic corps (b)

cultivos varios (empresa): Enterprise for several crops (c)

cumplir compromisos o un plan: to meet liabilities or a plan (c)

cumplir misión: to fulfill or undertake an internationalist mission (b)

cumpleaños colectivo: group birthday (a,c)

cuota de movilización: mobilization quota (b)

curso: a distancia: distance course (c)

    de actualización: refresher course (b,c)

    escolar: school term, school course (c)

    dirigido: guided independent studies, home course (c)

    de mínimo técnico: on-the-job training course; basic course (c)

    de nivelación: upgrading course (c)

    de perfeccionamiento: improvement course (c)

    de primeros auxilios: first aid course (c)

    de postgrado: post-graduate course (c)

    de reciclaje: brush-up course (c)

    de reorientación (para profesores que hacen una segunda especialidad): a second-major course (c)

    de seguimiento: follow-up course (c)

    de superación: upgrading course (c)

    de titulación: certification course (c)

    de verano: summer course (c)

    facultativo: elective course (a,c)

C.V.P. (empleado del Cuerpo de Vigilancia y Protección): watchman, security guard (c)

CH

chabacanería: slovenliness, sloppy work; shoddy work (a)

chaleco anti balas: bullet proof vest (a,c)

champola: custard apple shake (a)

charlista: lecturer (c)

chanchullo (negocios turbios): shady deals (a)

chapistería: body work (c)

chapucería: (por mala calidad del material): shoddy work (c)

(por mal trabajo): sloppy work (c)

charada: numbers racket (a)

Charangas de Bejucal: Bejucal Frolics (a)

charlatanería: charlatanry, charlatanism (a)

chatarra: scrap metal (a)

chequeo de emulación: emulation check up (c)

chequera de jubilado: pension check (a)

de círculo infantil: book of coupons (a)

chinchal: sweat shop, roach shop, a hole-in-the-wall shop (a,c)

chispa de tren (bebida de mala calidad): booze (a)

chivo (de fraude): pony, butt (a)

(barba): goatee (a)

(expiatorio): scapegoat (b)

choza: shack (a)

chuchería (comida): junk food (a)

chucho (transbordador de caña): cane loading station, cane reloading station (c)

D

damnificados: victims (of a disaster) (a)

Danza de los Millones: fat years (b)

dar de baja a un equipo: write it off, take it out of promotion (c)

defensa civil: civil defense (b)

deficiencias (fallos): shortcomings (b,c)

deprimir (precios): to drive down (prices) (b)

depurar responsabilidades: to fix individual responsibilities (c)

desafecto (dícese del que no comparte los lineamientos de la Revolución o su ideología): one who's gone sour on the Revolution (b)

desafío (reto): a tall order (b)

desalojo: eviction (b)

descanso retribuído: paid vacations (c)

descarga musical: jam session (a)

descogollador (de cana): topper (c)

despalillar tabaco: to strip tobacco (c)

descontinuado (equipo): discontinued (a,c)

desembarco del Granma: Granma landing (b)

desercion escolar: school drop-outs, drop-out rate (a,c)

desfile:

>del carnaval:Carnival Parade (c)
>
>Del Primero de Mayo: May Day Parade (c)
>
>Militar: military parade (c)
>
>de las antorchas: torchlight parade (c)
>
>de modas: fashion show (c)

despido: (de obreros) layoff

    (por sanción): to fire a worker (c)

despilfarro (de recursos materiales, etc.) : syphoning off (of resources, materials (c)

despliegue de fuerzas: show of forces (b)

despotismo ilustrado: enlightened despotism (b)

destacamento: detachment (a,b,c)

Destacamento Obrero de Acción Rápida: People's Defense Groups (b)

deuda externa: foreign debt (b)

desvío de un avión: to highjack a plane (b)

de recursos: misappropiation of resources (c)

día de la defensa: defense day (b)

día del esfuerzo decisivo: day of decisive effort (b)

día de la Rebeldía Nacional: National Rebellion Day (b)

día de haber: a day' s wages (a)

día hábil: lawful day (c)

día natural: calendar day (c)

diario de campaña: campaign diary (b)

dieta (dícese del dinero que se da a un trabajador para pagar comida, transporte y alojamiento):a per diem; an expense account (c)

diferencial azucarero: sugar differential (b)

diferendo: dispute, quarrel, differences (b)

diferido:

    a) en carrera universitaria: postponed (c)

    b) en transmisión: taped (c)

diplomado: certification course (a,c)

diputado: deputy (b,c)

directivas: directives (c)

Directorio Revolucionario: revolutionary directorate (b)

dirigente: leader (c)

disciplina laboral: work discipline (c)

disidente: dissident (b)

dispensarización (en el médico de familia): patient classification (a,c)

dispensarios rurales: rural dispensaries (a,c)

disposición combativa: combat readiness (a,b)

distensión (internacional): détente (b)

distinción: award (a,b,c)

diversionismo ideológico: ideological diversion (b)

divulgación: publicity (a,b)

divulgador: publicist (a,b)

división político-administrativa: political-administrative division (b)

doble moral: double standard (b)

documento rector: guiding document, model document (a,c)

Domingo Rojo: Red Sunday, Communist Sunday (b)

donación de órganos: donation of human organs (b)

       de sangre: blood donation (b)

       de un día de haber: donation of a day's wage (b)

drenaje parcelario: plot drainage (c)

E

economía de mercado: market economy (c)

edificios múltiples: apartment buildings, block of flats (a,c)

educación formal: correct behaviour, good manners (a)

educadora de Círculos Infantiles: day-care attendant (a)

efectivos (militares): troops, soldiers (b)

efectos electrodomésticos: household appliances (a,c)

efemérides: historical events (a,b)

Ejército Juvenil del Trabajo: Army of working youth (c)

Ejército Libertador: Liberation Army (b)

Ejército Rebelde: Rebel Army (b)

elaboración conjunta: (método pedagógico): guided discovery (c)

electores: constituents, voters (a,b)

embarazo precoz: early motherhood, teenager pregnancy (a)

empresa mayorista: wholesale enterprise (a,c)

    minorista: retail enterprise (a,c)

    mixta: joint venture (c)

empujador (caña): cowcatcher (c)

emulación al rojo vivo: red-hot emulation (b)

enarbolar las banderas: to hoist the colors (b)

encuentro de conocimientos: skill contest (c)

    (si es de ortografía): spelling bee (c)

encuesta: poll, survey (b)

en falta (dícese de un producto cuya distribución se ha interrumpido momentáneamente): out of stock (a)

enfoque: approach, outlook (a)

enlace (en lo militar): liaison (b)

enmascaramiento: camouflaging (b)

enseña nacional: national flag, Cuban flag (b)

ensilaje: (lugar): silo; (alimento): silage; (proceso): ensilage (c)

envío de mercancías: batch, lot, shipment, delivery (a)

escala industrial: on a large scale, mass production (c)

    salarial: wage scale (c)

escalafón: seniority system (c)

escalinata universitaria: University of Havana steps (a)

escalonado (referente a horarios o turnos de trabajo): staggered work shifts (a)

escoria (elementos desafectos al proceso revolucionario): scum (b)

escudo de armas: coat of arms (a)

escuela al campo (plan): the school goes to the country side (c)

    de iniciación deportiva (EIDE): school for basic sports training (c)

    superior de perfeccionamiento atlético (ESPA): school for advanced training of athletes (c)

    en el campo: school in the country (c)

    interarmas: interarms school (a)

    taller (para aprender un oficio): trade school (c)

    vocacional: polytechnic school (a)

especialista de primer grado: first degree specialist (c)

espíritu autocrítico: self-criticism

    combativo: fighting spirit

    de convivencia: spirit of camaraderie

de lucha: fighting spirit

de brigada: teamwork spirit

de sacrificio: selflessness (b)

esquematismo: hackneyed stereotypes (a,b)

estado mayor general: general staff; headquarters (b)

estado de sitio: state of siege (b)

estanco del tabaco: monopoly on tobacco (c)

estatutos del Partido: party statutes (b)

estímulo: incentive, prize (b)

estipendio (de padres a hijos): allowance. (a)

estructura de base: grass-roots structure (b)

exámenes de clasificación: placement exams (c)

de conciencia: honor system (c)

de ingreso: entrance exams (c)

de oposición: competitive exams (c)

de suficiencia: proficiency test (c)

parciales: mid-term exams (c)

excedente (de circulante) excess currency (a)

exigente (ser): to raise standards, to be demanding (a,b,c)

expediente (laboral) work record (c)

(acumulativo): academic record (a)

expedición del Gramma: Gramma expedition (b)

expedicionario: expeditionary (b)

explosión demográfica: demographic or population explosion, baby boom (a)

exposición de modas: fashion show (a)

extrema derecha: the far right (b)

extremo oriente: the far east (b)

F

facilismo: oversimplification; to take the easy way out; to look for easy solutions; to look for an easy approach (a,c)

factor de crecimiento epidérmico: epidermal growth factor (a)

factores: Political and mass organizations (b)

factura de cortesía: pro forma invoice (c)

facultad: school, faculty (a)

Facultad Obrero-Campesina: worker's and farmer's high school program (a,c)

faltante (después de un inventario): shortage, losses

fanatismo: fanaticism (b)

Federación de Mujeres Cubanas (FMC): Federation of Cuban Women (b,c)

Federación Cinológica de Cuba: Cuban Kennel Federation. (a).

federada: FMC member (a,c)

felpita (para el pelo): rubber band (a)

Feria de la Juventud: Youth Fair

      internacional del libro: international Book Fair

      de productos ociosos: idle product fair (a)

festejos: celebrations (a)

fichado: (por las autoridades) booked (a,c)

fidelidad: allegiance (b)

filas (del ejército o una organización): ranks (a,b)

filiación política: political affiliation; political leaning (b)

filial (sucursal): branch (c)

finalismo: en el estudio: cramming

      en el trabajo: an all-out-last-minute effort; eleventh-hour

effort (a)

fincas: farms (a)

fisminutos: five-minute gym practice (a)

flota pesquera: fishing fleet (c)

foco de crisis: world hot spot (b)

      de tensión: hotbed of tension (b)

fonda (comedor): dirty spoon; joint (a)

Fondo Cubano de Bienes Culturales: Cuban Cultural Foundation, Foundation of cultural assets, Cuban arts and crafts Foundation (b)

      de tiempo: time bank (c)

      monetario: monetary fund (c)

fonoteca: music library (a)

fototeca: archives (a,c)

forense: coroner, examiner (c)

forjadores del futuro: builders of the future (c)

formación integral: all -round training (a,c)

formalismo: sheer formalism (b)

formas terminadas: pharmaceutical forms (c)

formulismo: resorting to hackneyed formulas (b)

fosas colectivas (en el cementerio): family graves (a)

fosas comunes (en la guerra): mass graves (a)

Fragua Martiana: Monument to José Martí in La Punta Fortress (b)

fraude académico: cheating (a)

      en elecciones: bogus elections, sham elections (b,c)

frente femenino: women's section (c)

frigorífico: cold storage plant or room; refrigerator ship, meat locker (c)

fruticuba: fruit store (a)

fuente de recaudación: income spinner (a,c)

fuga de capitales: flight of capitals (b)

funcionario: official, public official (b,c)

frutas selectas: choice fruits (a,c)

frutos menores: truck farming (a,c)

Fuerzas Armadas Revolucionarias (FAR): Revolutionary Armed Forces (b,c)

fuerzas de choque: Strike forces (b,c)

Fuerzas Guardafronteras del Ministerio del Interior: ministry of the interior's border patrol (b)

fuerzas productivas: productive forces (c)

fuerza de trabajo: work force (c)

fullero: trickster (a)

función única: a one-off show (a)

G

gaceta oficial: official gazette (a)

galardón: award, banner (b)

gallardete: banner, streamer (a)

ganancias inventadas: trumped-up profits (c)

garrotero (usurero): loan shark (a)

gas licuado: bottled gas (a)

    de la calle: city gas service (a)

gasolina especial: unleaded gasoline (a)

gastronomía: food services (a,c)

genocidio: mass murder, genocide (b)

General de División: division general (b)

Generación del Centenario: Generation of the cenntenial (b)

gesta: action

    del Moncada: attack on the Moncada garrison (b)

gestiones en empresas: management (c)

    del Grupo de Contadora: efforts or negotiations sponsored by the contadora group (b)

gimnasia laboral: work gymnastic (c)

gimnasia matutina: P.T. (physical training) (a,c)

golpe de estado: coup d'etat (b)

granjas: state-owned farms (c)

grupos de aficionados al arte (como observadores): art appreciation group (a)

    (como participantes): art amateur groups (a,c)

Grupo de Contadora: Contadora Group (c)

Grupo de Experimentación Sonora del ICAIC: ICAIC Experimental Sound Group (a)

grupúsculos: fringe groups (b)

guaposo (delincuente): hoodlum (a,c)

guarandinga: rural bus (a)

guarapo: sugar cane juice (a)

guardaespalda: body guard (a,b)

guardafronteras: border patrol (b)

guardia:

> **estar de guardia**: to be on duty
>
> **cuerpo de guardia en un hospital**: emergency ward
>
> **cuerpo de guardia en lo militar**: guard room (b,c)
>
> **vieja**: to do trash duty, clean-up squad, to police
>
> the ground (a,c)

guateque campesino: country dance (a,c)

guerra de desgaste: war of attrition (b)

> **de guerrillas**: guerrilla warfare (b)
>
> **de las galaxias**: star war (b)
>
> **de los Diez Años**: ten years' war (b)
>
> **de todo el pueblo**: the war of all the people (b)

guerrillero: guerrilla fighter, partisan (b)

guía de pioneros: pioneers' guide (b)

gusanos (desafectos): gusanos (b)

gusanera: counterrevolutionary rabble (b)

H

hacendados: big land owners, latifundist (b,c)

hacienda: country estate (a)

hago constar: certification, doctor's note, sick note (a,c)

Hasta la Victoria Siempre: Ever onward to victory (b)

heladería: ice-cream parlor (a)

hemeroteca (catálogo y existencia de las publicaciones periódicas): morgue (c)

héroe anónimo: unsung hero (b,c)

    Nacional (José Martí): National hero (b)

    del Trabajo: hero of labor (c)

    del Moncada (bandera): Hero of the Moncada banner (c)

    de la zafra: hero of the harvest (c)

higiene y seguridad del trabajo: safety and hygiene on the job (c)

hilo directo: hot line (a,b)

hogar materno: home for expectant mothers (a)

hoja de ruta: way bill (c)

hoja de vuelo: flight plan (c)

homólogo (dícese del que comparte iguales funciones): counterpart (b,c)

horario abierto (para docentes): flexible hours or schedule (a,c)

horario deslizante: over time (c)

hora militar: military time (b)

horario rotativo: to work flextime (c)

horario de verano: day-light saving time(a)

hospital clínico-quirúrgico: clinical-surgical hospital (a)

de campaña: field hospital (b)

de día: Day-care hospital (a)

docente: teaching hospital (a,c)

rural: rural hospital (a)

huelga de brazos caídos: a slow-down (b)

huso horario: time zone (a)

I

idoneidad: (para una plaza laboral):appropriateness (c)

impermeabilizar (techos): to waterproof the roofs (c)

incidencias: highlights (a)

incidencias laborales: work discipline (c)

indicadores: indexes (c)

indicadores directivos: executive indicators or indexes (c)

índice académico: G.P.A. (General Performance Average) (a)

índice de rechazo: (botellas que no tienen comercialización y deben retornar al proceso productivo): non-recycling of bottles (c)

indocumentado: illegal alien,people lacking papers (b)

inflar globos: (alterar cifras) to trump up figures or targets (a)

informe central: main report (b)

ingenio (azucarero): sugar mill (c)

ingerencista (política): interventionist (policy) (b)

ingreso domiciliario: (referente a un paciente): home care; treatment at home (b)

ingresos brutos: gross incomes (c)

Ingresos inflados: overblown incomes (c)

Inquietudes artísticas: artistic leanings (c)

instituir (una orden o distinción): to confer upon (b)

Instituto de la Demanda Interna: Institute for Market Research and Consumers' Guidance (a,b)

instituciones de seguro: insurance institutions (c)

inseminación artificial: artificial insemination (c)

insumos en la industria: imports, consumables (c)

      en la agricultura: materials and equipments (c)

intercambio desigual: unequal terms of trade, unequal exchange (b)

interconsulta: medical assessment (c)

interferir (por una emisora): to jam (b)

interino (director): temporary (director) (c)

intermediario: middleman, go-between (b,c)

internacionalismo: internationalism (b)

internado (escuela): boarding school (c)

interrupto: worker temporarily laid off with 70% of payment (c)

intervención (al hablar):

    (de una persona relevante): address, remark (b)

    (de menor relevancia): statement (b)

intransigencia: intransigence, uncompromising attitude (a,b,c)

invasión mercenaria: mercenary invasion (b)

inventario ocioso: idle stock (c)

Isla de la Juventud: Isle of Youth (b)

Isla de Pinos: Isle of Pines (b)

J

jaiberos: cane loaders (c)

jardín botánico: Botanical garden (a)

jardín de la infancia: Nursery school, kindergarten (a)

jefatura de movilización: Mobilization headquarters (b)

jefe: chief, boss

    de brigada: brigade chief

    de lote (agricultura): foreman (b,c)

    de compañia (militar): company chief (b)

    de departamento: head of department (c)

    de estado: head of state (b)

    de obra: foreman (c)

    de personal: chief of personnel (c)

    de redacción: editor in chief (c)

    de sector: sector chief (b)

    técnico: chief technician (c)

jerarquizar: to set priorities for (a,c)

jinetero (proxeneta para obtención de divisas): hooker, pimp (c)

jinetera: groupie (a,c)

jornada de actividades (por una fecha determinada): Day, week, month in honor of, solidarity campaign (b)

    de corte de caña: cane cutting session (c)

    de 45 días: 45-day rally (c)

    de fin de año: year-end work drive (a,c)

    de girón: Girón fortnight agricultural drive (b)

    especial: special workdays (c)

    guerrillera: guerrilla work rally,guerrilla workdays (b)

laboral: workday (c)

productiva: productive activity day,productive work session (c)

de solidaridad: solidarity campaign (b)

de trabajo voluntario: voluntary work session (c)

juez lego: lay judge (c)

junta de coordinación, ejecución e inspección: board of

coordination, execution and inpection (c)

central de planificación:(JUCEPLAN) Central planning

board (c)

de planificación física: physical planning board (c)

electoral: electoral board (a)

Juramento de Baraguá: Oath of Baraguá (b)

jurar la bandera: to swear allegiance to flag (b)

jurista: jurist (c)

L

llamado al Servicio militar: call to military service (b)

lanzamiento (de un libro o disco al mercado y por primera vez): launching, presentation (a)

lavado de dinero: money laundering (b)

lavatín: laundromat, laundry (a)

levantamiento:

       a) sublevación: uprising (b)

       b) de viviendas: survey (a,c)

ley:

       a) contra la vagancia: law against vagrancy (c)

       b) de obediencia debida y punto final: (para los militares en Chile): law of limited responsability for the military (b)

       c) general de la vivienda: general housing law (a)

       d) de Reforma Agraria: Agrarian Reform law (c)

       e) de Reforma Urbana: Urban Reform law (a)

       f) de Ajuste Cubano: Cuban Adjustment Act (b)

libreta de abastecimiento: ration card, ration book (a)

libretazo (en nuestro contexto familiar tomar decisiones a título personal): to take undue liberties (b,c)

licencia de maternidad: maternity leave (c) to overstep authority (said of chiefs) (b,c)

Limpia del Escambray: Escambray mop-up drive (b)

lineamientos: guidelines (b)

listos para vencer (LPV): fit to win (b)

Lonja del Comercio: Commercial Exchange (c)

lucha:

  a) contra bandidos:fight against bands of

  counterrevolutionaries (a,b)

  b) clandestina: underground struggle (b)

  c) contra el delito: crime prevention, a crackdown on

  crime (b)

  d) contra el sedentarismo:struggle against obesity and a

  sedentary style of life (a)

  e) guerrillera: guerrilla warfare (b)

lucro: lust for gain, profit-oriented motive (c)

ludoteca: game arcade (a)

lumpen: lumpen (c)

M

maceta (especulador de mercado negro): profiteer (c)

machetero: canecutter (c)

machismo: male chauvinism; male superiority (a,b)

machista: male chauvinist, macho (a,b)

maestros ambulantes: home teachers (a)

maestros emergentes: emergency teachers,crash course teachers (a,c)

manifestación (de protesta): demonstration (b)

mantenimiento (a un equipo): upkeep, maintenace (c)

mano a mano (generalizado para encuentros de artistas o profesionales de un mismo género o actividad): double-header show (a)

mano de obra: (confección, hechura) workmanship (b)

    (fuerza laboral) man power (c)

marca estatal de calidad: quality seal (c)

marco (dentro del marco de): within the framework of (a)

Marcha de las antorchas: torchlight parade

    candlelight parade (b)

Marcha del Pueblo Combatiente: The People's March (b)

masa cárnica: meat paste (a)

matutino (acto que se realiza en las escuelas antes de comenzar las clases por la mañana): home room (a,b)

mechado (alumno estudioso): culture vulture, bunsen, plugger (b)

medicina alternativa: alternative medicine (a)

medicina del trabajo: occupational health (a,c)

Medicina General Integral: comprehensive general medicine (a,b)

medicina legal: coroner's office; legal medicine; medical examiner, forensics (c)

medicina preventiva: preventive medicine (a,c)

medicina verde: green medicine (a)

médico de la familia: Family Doctor, Community Doctor (a)

medio:

>   a) básico: state-owned facility (a,c)

>   b) de difusión masiva: mass media (a,c)

>   c) ocioso: idle facility (c)

>   d) de propaganda: means of dissemination (b)

mención honorífica: honorable mention (a)

mensajero: delivery man (c)

menú dirigido: a set menu (a,c)

mercachifles: profiteering go-betweens (c)

Mercado Libre Campesino: farm market for unrationed produce (a)

mercado paralelo:

>   a) en lenguaje financiero: free market transactions (a)

>   b) de productos liberados: market for unrationed goods (a)

mercado concentrador: wholesale produce distributor (a)

mercanchiflismo: wheeling and dealing (c)

merolicos: street peddlers, street vendors, hawkers, hucksters (c)

merendero: snack bar (a)

mesada (mensualidad): allowance (a)

mesa redonda: round table (b)

mesa sueca: smorgasbord, buffet table (a)

meta (de trabajo): work goal (c)

microbrigadas: minibrigades (c)

Microcirugía Ocular en Serie: Eye consecutive microsurgery (a)

miembro:

       a) efectivo: full member

       b) suplente: alternate member (b,c)

       c) actualizado (en cotización): paid-up member (c)

Milicias de Tropas Territoriales: Territorial Troop Militia (b)

miliciano: militia, militia member (b)

militancia: militancy, membership (b)

militante: militant (b)

       a) comunista: communist party member (b)

mínimo técnico:

       (antes de empezar a trabajar): a basic course (c)

       (mientras trabaja): on the job training (c), on the job

       training course; a basic course (c)

mirador: (punto de observación) lookout tower, lookout point (a,c)

misión internacionalista: internationalist mission (b)

mitin:

       a) de repudio: protest meeting, repudiation meeting (b)

       b) relámpago: flash meeting (b,c)

modalidad libre (para un doctorado): distant mode, free mode (c)

módulos: annexes, packages (c)

moneda libremente convertible: hard currency (b,c)

montaje (de industrias): installation (c)

monumento nacional: national monument, national landmark. (b)

movilización: mass mobilization, rally (b)

movimiento (social):

      a) de áreas protegidas: safety areas movement (c)

      b) de la Nueva Trova: the New Trobadour movement, the New Song Movement (a,b)

      c) de avanzada: avant garde movement (c)

      d) obrero: labor movement (c)

      e) de Innovadores y Racionalizadores: movement of innovators and rationalizers (c)

      f) de Madres Combatientes: fighting mothers movement, parent teachers association (a)

      g) vanguardista: vanguard movement (c)

      h) de tierra: earth-moving operations (c)

multi mueble: wall unit (a)

multioficio: multiskill, multi task job (c)

municipio: municipality (a,c)

mural (para noticias y efemérides): bulletin board (c)

música indirecta: piped-in music (a)

N

nacionalización: nationalization (b)

nave (almacén): warehouse (c)

(avícola): poultry shed (c)

(ovina): sheep shed (c)

(porcina): hog shed (c)

(si es con techo semicircular de metal) quonset hut (c):

nivel:

a) de base: grass-roots level (b)

b) de escolaridad: scholastic level (a)

no apto: (para el servicio militar) 4-F (a)

nomenclatura (definición de tareas que requiere una plaza

determinada): job slotting (c)

nómina: pay roll (c)

normalización: standardization (c)

norma: labor standard (c)

normador: normsetter, standardsetter (c)

normados (productos normados):

a) por la libreta: rationed products (a)

b) con normas en la producción: standardized products

(c)

normalización: standardization (c)

normativa: regulation,norms, procedures (c)

notaría: justice of the peace (a,c)

núcleo (del PCC): party cell, party nucleus (b)

O

objeto de obra: construction target (c)

obras:

a) de choque: top-priority tasks (c)

b) industriales: industrial works (c)

c) sociales: community projects (b,c)

obrero calificado: skilled worker (c)

ofensiva revolucionaria: revolutionary drive (b)

oferta-demanda: supply-demand (a)

oficiales, clases y soldados: officers, noncommisioned officers and soldiers (b)

oficial operativo: officer of the day (c)

oficial de la reserva: reserve officer (b)

oleoducto: pipelines (a,c)

olla colectiva: soup line (b)

onda (marchar acorde a las manifestaciones de la moda): trend, a trendy person (a)

opción cero: zero option (b)

optimizar: to make the best possible use of; to optimize (a,c)

orden (distinción): award, order (b,c)

organismos:

a) de masa: mass organization (b)

b) estatal: state agency (b,c)

órganos:

a) locales del Poder Popular: People's Power bodies (a,b)

b) de la Seguridad del Estado: State Security Agencies (b)

    c) del estado: agency, body (b)

    d) de gobierno: ruling body (b)

organismos (del estado): state agencies, government agencies (b)

organograma: organization chart (c)

organoponico: organoponic (a,c)

orientación (directriz): guideline (b,c)

orientación profesional: guidance counselling (c)

orientador (de círculos de estudio): discussion leader (b)

    (vocacional): guidance counsellor (a,c)

orientadora:

    a) de Salud: health counselor (c)

    b) rural: rural counselor (c)

P

Pabellón Cuba: Cuba Pavillion (a)

pacotilla: (artículos de poco valor) trinkets, knick knacks (a)

padres ejemplares en la educación: exemplary parents

in education (a)

padrinos de escuela: school sponsors (a)

padrinos de alumnos deficientes: coach, tutor (a,b)

palabra de orden: watchword (a,b)

Palacio:

> a) de la Artesanía: House of Handicrafts; Handicraft
>
> Palace (a)
>
> b) de las Convenciones: International Conference Center
>
> (a)
>
> c) del Segundo Cabo: Palace of the Second in Command,
>
> Intendencia Palace (a)
>
> d) de los matrimonios: Wedding Palace (a)
>
> e) de los pioneros :Pioneer Palace (a)
>
> f) de la Revolucion:Palace of the Revolution (b)
>
> g) Presidencial: Presidential Palace (b)

palangre: long line trawling (c)

palenque: settlement (a)

pancarta: placard (b)

pantrista: pantry attendant (c)

pañoleta de pionero: neckerchief (a,b)

papel recuperado: (si está escrito): used paper

> (si está procesado): recycled paper (c)

paralizar: (una construcción): held up

> (un trámite): paralyzed

> (una situación): stalemated

> (un salario): frozen wages

> (un carro): held up

parasitismo (actitud negativa): freeloading (b)

parcelero: wildcat farmer (c)

Parlamento Obrero: Workers' Parliament (b)

paro laboral: work stoppage (c)

Parrandas de Remedios: Remedios Revels (a)

párvulo: toddler (a)

pasantía: practicum, practical training (a,c)

pasarela: (en desfile de modas) catwalk, runway (a,c)

pasar el cepillo: (un cantante o artista): to pass the hat around (a)

> (en la iglesia): to take up the collection, to pass the alms

> man (a)

Paseo:

> a) del Malecón: seafront drive (a)

> b) del Prado: Prado promenade (a)

paso de avance: stride forward (b)

Paso de los Vientos (Barlovento): windward (a)

patana: flatboat, flat-bottomed boat (a,c)

patentizar: to make evident (a)

Patrimonio Cultural de la Humanidad: world heritage (a)

Patrullas click: Click Brigades (a,c)

Patrulla fluvial: River Rescue (c)

paz interna: domestic peace (b)

pedraplén: stone causeway (c)

peinar (una zona): to finish a zone (a)

        (buscar a un delincuente): to comb (a)

peligrosidad (riesgos de trabajo): hazardous work conditions (c)

pelotear (transferir una responsabilidad): to pass the buck (c)

pellizco: (para el pelo) barrette (a)

pensión alimenticia:

        (a un niño, en caso de divorcio): child support payment

        (a,b)

        (a una mujer en caso de divorcio) alimony (a,b)

peña:

        a) literaria: literary circle (a)

        b) del tango: tango club (a)

        c) del humor: humor club (a)

peón: laborer, worker (c)

pepillo: up to date, in fashion, sweet girl, sweet boy (a)

pequeño agricultor: small farmer (c)

perfeccionamiento (planes y programas):

        improvement (plans and programs) (c)

perfil (laboral): profile

        a) ancho: broad profile (c)

        b) estrecho: narrow profile (c)

permuta: house swap (a)

período especial: special period (a,b,c)

peritaje médico: team medical examination (a)

pertinencia social: social influence (a)

pesquisaje: screening (c)

picadillo extendido: mince with additives (a)

pico eléctrico: peak consumption hour (a)

pie forzado (en la música campesina): a forced rhyme (a)

pienso líquido: liquid fodder (c)

piezas:

      a) de repuesto: spare parts (a,c)

      b) de recuperación: repaired parts

pilotaje: pilot plans, on a experimental basis (c)

piloto (cervecera): outdoor beer stands (a)

pim pam pum: roll away bed (a)

pincho (dirigente que hace ostentación y abuso de su cargo): big shot (c)

piña (grupo de personas): clique

pioneros exploradores: pioneer scouts (a)

pipa (camión de agua): cistern truck (a,c)

piquera (de taxis): taxi stand (a)

piratear (plagiar): to lift, to plagiarize (a)

pistero: gas station attendant (c)

pizarra humana: card section (a)

pizzería: pizza parlor, pizza place (a)

placita: vegetables market (a,c)

plan:

      a) plan de la calle: recreation plan (a)

      b) plan jaba: special shopping plan for working women (a)

     c) plan tareco: junk collection plan (a)

     d) plan predespacho: pick-up service (a)

planificación: planning (c)

planta de beneficio (de minerales): dressing plant (c)

planta de energía: power plant (c)

plantas saneadas: pathogen-free plants (c)

planteamiento: statement, proposal, suggestion (a,b)

plantilla (de un centro de trabajo): staff (c)

     (para ponerse zapatos): ped. (a)

     (tamaño del pie): outline of the foot (a)

plantilla inflada: overstaffing (c)

plataforma insular: insular shelf (a,c)

Plataforma Programática: Programatic Platform (b)

Playa Girón: Bay of Pigs (b)

Plaza:

     a) de la Catedral: Cathedral Square (a)

     b) de la Revolución: Revolution Square (b)

     c) Roja: Workers' Plaza; Red Square (c)

     d) laboral o para la universidad: post, position, opening

     (c)

plenaria: plenary session (b)

pleno: plenum, plenary meeting (b)

plustrabajo: extra work, overtime (c)

población flotante : floating population (a)

poder adquisitivo: purchasing power (a)

Poder Local: local government (b)

Poeta Nacional: National Poet (a,b)

polaínas: gaiters (a)

policía acostado: speed bump (a,c)

policlínico: polyclinic (a)

polígono: practice grounds, parade grounds (b)

Política de las Cañoneras: Gunboat Diplomacy (b)

politiquería: sham politicking (b)

polo cientifico del oeste: western scientific complex (c)

ponencia: paper (c)

ponente:

      a) en un evento: speaker (c)

      b) en una disputa legal: arbitrator (c)

ponina (colecta): fund raising, a whip round (a)

por orden de llegada: first come, first served (a,c)

por sustitución reglamentaria: acting director (c)

portadores energéticos: sources of energy (c)

posta médica: medical post (a)

posta sanitaria: first-aid station (a,b)

post-guardia: off duty (c)

potencia médica: medical power (b)

práctica:

      a) docente: teaching practice (c)

      b) de tiro: target practice (a,c)

      c) de producción: in-service training (c)

precarista: squatter (c)

preciosismo (con detalles): hair splitting (a,c)

premio flaco: booby prize (a)

premio gordo: to hit the jackpot (a)

preparación combativa: combat training (b)

presidio modelo: model prison (b)

prevención social: social prevention (b,c)

primas (estímulo material): bonus (c)

primer expediente (de un curso): valedictorian (a,c)

Primer Ministro: Prime Minister (b)

Primer Secretario del Partido: First Secretary of the Party (b)

primeriza (embarazada): first-time mother (a)

Primero de Mayo: May Day (b,c)

priorizar: to set priorities for, prioritize (a,c)

proceso:

      a) de crecimiento (UJC o PCC): growth process (b)

      b) de rectificación: rectification process (b)

productividad: productivity (c)

productos:

      a) liberados: non rationed products (a)

      b) ociosos: idle products, unused products (a)

profesor guía: teacher guide (a,c)

programa de tránsito: program which is being phased out (c)

promoción de salud: health promotion (a,b)

promocionismo: (actuación o principio que tiende a promover sin la calidad o los requisitos debidos): penchant for passing students (b)

promotor: (se utiliza para designar al que promueve o impulsa una actividad dada): champion (b,c)

protección e higiene: work safety and hygiene (c)

protección del trabajo: work safety (c)

proyecto (de ley): draft, bill (b)

    (llave en mano): turn -key project (c)

proyecto por producto (si es uno por uno): project for product (c)

    (si son 3,4 ó 5 por uno) : project per product (c)

prueba:

    a) citológica: Pap smears, Pap test (a)

    b) de eficiencia física: physical fitness tests (a,b)

    c) de fuego (vencer un ejercicio, situación o circunstancia difícil): trial by fire (a)

    d) de ingreso (a la Universidad): A-1 test, S.A.test (standard aptitude test) (a)

    e) dinámica (en elecciones): a dry run (a)

    f) en seco (para censo de población): a dry run (a,b)

puesto:

    a) de dirección: leadership post (b)

    b) de mando: command post (b,c)

    c) de trabajo: work place, work site (c)

    d) de viandas y hortalizas: stall (a,c)

puericultura (visitas de médico a un bebé): well-baby visits (a)

punta de lanza (utilizar y escudarse tras algo o alguien con determinado objetivo): spearhead (b)

punto:

    a) de control: check point (b)

    b) de leche: dairy (a)

c) de recogida (para becados): pick-up point (a)

puntualidad: promptness (c)

Q

quincalla: notions shop (a)

quinquenal (plan): five-year plan (a)

quinquenio: quinquenium, five-year period (a)

R

racionalizar (plazas en un centro de trabajo): to reduce the staff; to reduce the pay-roll; to optimize, downsizing (c)

racionamiento: rationing (a,c)

Radio Base: p-a system (public address system) (c)

ramo: field, branch of trade, line of business, division or part of an art or science (c)

rancheador:

> a) de esclavos: runaway slave catcher (a)

> b) de animales: bounty hunter (a)

rastro (de chatarra): junk yard (a)

realengo: unappropriated land (a,c)

rebambaramba: free-for-all (a)

recalificación: retraining (c)

receso escolar: mid-term break (a)

recinto ferial: fair grounds (a)

recta final: homestretch (a)

recuperación de bienes del Estado: Agency for the recovery of assets (b)

recuperación de materia prima: collecting of bottles, stamps, paper, tubes for recycling (a,c)

recursos humanos: human resources (c)

red comercial: retail trade network (a)

reducir plantillas: downsize, downsizing (c)

reforma:

> a) Agraria: Agrarian reform (b,c)

> b) salarial: wage reform (c)

refuerzo (de ómnibus): extra service (a,c)

   (de policía): backup (b,c)

refugios (para la evacuación): air-raid shelters (b)

regional: district level (b)

registro farmacéutico: licensing (c)

relevar la guardia: to spell the watch (c)

relevo (en el trabajo social o turnos contínuos): relief, substitute (c)

remesa: remittance (a)

rendimiento académico: academic standing (a)

renegociar (la deuda externa): to reschedule the foreign debt (b)

renglón económico: export item, line for export, branch of production (c)

rentabilidad: profitability; income yield capacity, economically viable (b)

repentistas: (de música campesina) improvisers (a,c)

reposición: (a)

   a) de equipos electrodomésticos: to trade in a set on a new one

   b) de películas: a re-run (a)

   c) en el teatro: a re-stage (a)

república mediatizada: compromised republic (b)

rescate de tradiciones: revival of traditions (a,c)

reserva laboral: workers' pool (c)

reservista: reservist (b)

resguardo (espiritual): hoyo, moyo, charm (a)

respuestas calibradas: scaled responses (c)

retención escolar: prevention of school dropouts (a,c)

retrato hablado: identikit portrait, identikit picture, police sketch (a)

reubicar (trabajadores): to relocate (c)

reunionismo: tendency to hold too many meetings (c)

revalorización (en exámenes): re-sit test (a)

revendedor: hawkers, hucksters (de boletos o tickets); scalper (a)

revés (contratiempo): setback (a,b)

Revolución de Octubre: October Revolution (b)

rezagos del pasado: hangovers from the past (b)

rincón del humor: humor club (a)

Rincón Martiano: a bust of Martí (a)

riñonera (cangurita): fanny pack; money belt (a)

rivalidar (título): to revalidate (c)

robo de cerebros: brain drain (b)

rodeo: rodeo (a)

ronda (recorrido): beat (a,b)

ropa reciclada (usada): used clothes (a)

S

sabado corto: non-working Saturday (b)

> Small bottle of rum (a)

sala:

> a) de cuidados intensivos: intensive care ward (a)
>
> b) de video: video club (c)
>
> c) polivalente: multipurpose auditorium, sports facility (c)

salidas ilegales: illegal departures (b)

salideros: (de agua o gas):leaking pipes, a gas leakage (a,c)

saludar:

> a) celebrar: to hold activities in honor of; to celebrate (a)
>
> b) dar la bienvenida a: to welcome the visit of (c)

salud pública: public health (a)

salto cualitativo: qualitative leap (a,b)

sanear finanzas: To tidy up finances (c)

sanidad vegetal: plant protection (c)

sapear: to jinx or jynx (a,c)

sapo (rompegrupo; persona indeseable)(en países caribeños): limer (a)

seccional (determinado nivel de una organización): section committee (b)

sección sindical: trade union (c)

secretariado ejecutivo: executive secretariat (c)

secretario general:

> a) de una organización internacional: secretary general
>
> b) de una organización nacional: general secretary (b,c)

sede: venue; host country; host center, headquarters, site (b)

seguidores (adictos a una causa): adherents to (b)

segunda vuelta (en una elección): a runoff election (b)

Segundo Frente Frank País: Frank Pais Second Front (b)

seguridad de valores: Brinks truck (c)

seguridad social: social security (a)

seleccionado juvenil: youth representation (a)

selectiva de béisbol: baseball championship (a)

semi-internado: day-boarding school (a)

señalamientos (críticas o sugerencias): remarks; criticisms (a,b)

serial (de T.V): T.V. serial; soap opera (a)

serigrafía: silk screens (a,c)

servicentro: gas station (a)

servicios comunales: community services (a)

servicio de mensajero: Food-shopping service (a)

Servicio Militar Activo: Active Military Service (a)

Servicio Militar Obligatorio: Compulsory Military Service (a)

servicio social: social service (c)

símbolos patrios: national symbols (a,b)

simulacro de evacuación: practice evacuation (b)

    de incendio: fire drill (b)

    de prácticas militares: simulated attack (b)

    en seco: (para censo de población): a dry run (a)

sin tregua: without respite, without letup (a,b) (Véase tregua)

sindicalista: trade unionist (c)

sistema electro-energético: national power grid (c)

sobrecumplir (un plan o norma): to overfulfill (b)

sobreestadía: (de un buque) demurrhage (c)

sociolismo (actitud negativa): favoritism, cronyism (b)

solapín (identificación personal dentro de un ámbito dado; credencial): name badge; I.D. badge, name tag (c)

solar (cuartería): tenement (a)

solidaridad: solidarity (a,b)

sonajero: Chinese chimes; mobile; wind chimes (a)

sumarísimo (juicio): summary trial (b)

superación:

> a) cursos: upgrading courses (c)

> b) planes: in-service plans (c)

sustentabilidad: sustainability (a,c)

T

tabla gimnástica: mass gymnastics display, coreographed gymnastics (c)

tandem: mill train (c)

tanque pensante: thinking tank (b)

taquilla: (a,c)

       a) para dejar recados: pigeon hole

       b) para cambiarse de ropa: locker

       c) en el cine o teatro: box office

tasas de interés: interest rates (b)

tea incendiaría: incendiary torch (b,c)

técnico medio: intermediate-level technician (c)

tecnicismos: technicalities (c)

tecnología de punta: cutting-edge technology (b)

telenovela: soap opera (a)

teleprofesor: teleprofessor (a)

tendencias negativas: negative trends or tendencies (b)

terapia intensiva polivalente: multipurpose intensive care (a,c)

Terminales Mambisas: Shipping Agency (a)

terraplen: enbankment (c)

terreno (visitas del medico de la familia a los pacientes que este trata directamente): house calls (a)

tertulia: literary get- together;social club meeting (a)

tienda comisionista: second hand store (a)

tiempo de vida: (en alimentos) shelf life (c)

tiempo muerto:dead season (c)

tienda comisionista: second-hand store (a)

timbiriche: stand, kiosk (a)

timbiricheo: (negocios no autorizados): wheeling and dealing (a)

tinajones: clay jars (a)

titimaníaco (en países de habla caribeña): sugar daddy (a)

titular

    a) cuenta de ahorro: holder (a)

    b) de deportes: champion (c)

    c) categoría docente o cientifica: Full Professor, Full Researcher (c)

    d) ministro: minister (b,c)

toma de conciencia (política): political awakening; development of awareness (b)

toma de poder (de un Presidente): inauguration (b)

tope (deportivo): sports meet; match (c)

toque de cazuela: pots and pan protest (b)

toque de queda: curfew (b)

torcedor de tabacos: cigar maker (c)

tormenta de ideas: brainstorm, brainstorming (a)

torneos intramurales: intramural tourneys (a)

torpedo: check list (a,c)

trabajador excedente (en general): excess worker (c)

    por una sanción: fired, dismissed (c)

trabajador social: social worker (c)

trabajador por cuenta propia: self-employed worker (en el caso de un fotógrafo o un periodista: a freelance (photographer; writer; journalist or reporter) (c)

trabajador contratado: part-time worker (c)

trabajo productivo: productive work (b,c)

trabajo voluntario: voluntary work (b,c)

tramitador: person in charge of paperwork in a work center (c)

trámites: pre-requisites, paperwork, running around (c)

trapicheo (tráfico no autorizado de mercancías): trafficking (a)

tratamiento focal: fumigation (a,c)

trayectoria revolucionaria: revolutionary record; revolutionary path; revolutionary history (b)

tregua (para terminar la guerra): truce (si no se pretende terminar): respite. (Véase sin tregua)

  Tregua Fecunda: The necessary respite (b)

tribuna antimperialista: anti-imperialist tribunal

tribuna abierta: public address platform.

  presidencial: presiding stand

  plataforma: speaker's rostrum (b)

tribunal para exámenes: examining commission, board of

  examiners (a)

  popular: people's court (b)

  revolucionario: revolutionary court (b)

tridente (salarial): salary scale level (c)

triunfalismo: empty boasting (b)

Trocha (Júcaro-Morón): Júcaro-Morón line of forts (b)

trocheros: trailblazers (c)

tronado (sancionado): busted (b)

tropas especiales: elite troops; special troops (b)

tropas de choque: shock troops (b)

tropas de pioneros exploradores: pioneer scouting troops (a)

trovador: troubador (a)

túneles populares: air-raid shelters (a,b)

tupamaros (cigarros): hand-rolled cigarettes (a)

turno rotativo: staggered work shift (c)

U

ubicación laboral: assignment, placement (c)

unidad: (c)

      a) militar: military unit

      b) modelo: model unit

      c) móvil: mobile unit

      d) presupuestada: budgeted unit (c)

uniforme: (de soldado o militar): fatigues (b,c)

unión: (b,c)

      a) de Jóvenes Comunistas: Young Communist League; Young Communist Union

      b) de Escritores y Artistas de Cuba: Union of Cuban Artists and Writers

      c) de Juristas de Cuba: National Union of Jurists of Cuba

      d) de Periodistas de Cuba: Journalists' Union of Cuba

      e) Unión de Pioneros de Cuba: Union of Cuban Pioneers

unión consensual:

      a) one's significant other: My significant other.

      b) common law marriage

      c) P.O.S.S.L.Q.[1] (a)

      (Person of opposite sex sharing living quarters)

      Exs.: (He, She) is my POSSLQ

      This is the place where we POSSLQ.

      We're not married; we're posslqued.

      I'm posslquing with her.

---

1.   MILWAUKEE JOURNAL, June 19th, 1980.

universalización (de la enseñanza): universalization of teaching (b)

usuario: (a)

      a) en general: user

      b) en una tienda: customer, client

      c) en un restaurante: patron

      d) en un vehículo: passenger

usufructuario oneroso: renter (a,b)

V

vacas:

    a) flacas (años difíciles): lean years (b)

    b) gordas (años prósperos): years of plenty (b)

    c) sagrada (personalidad o entidad intocable desde el

    punto de vista crítico): sacred cow (a)

validación: evaluation, validation (c)

valija de la amistad: solidarity gift collection point (a)

valija diplomática: diplomatic pouch (c)

veda: closed season (a)

veintena guerrillera: three-week guerrilla, work stint (c)

velada:

    a) cultural: evening performance, cultural evening (a)

    b) solemne: solemn ceremony (b)

viales: roads (c)

vías no formales: informal kindergarten (a)

viceministro: deputy minister (b)

vicepresidente: vice-president (b)

videoteca: video library (a)

vigencia: timeliness, applicability, indefeasibility, lasting validity (b,c)

vigilancia:

    a) en general: watch, vigilance (b)

    b) cederista: C.D.R. vigilance (b)

    c) epidemiológica (pesquisaje): epidemiological

    screening, epidemiological surveillance (a)

    d) revolucionaria: revolutionary vigilance (b)

villa de salud: health spa (a)

vinculación (a una norma de trabajo):

> a) para los obreros: to do piecework; to be on a piecework basis (c)

> b) para la administración: to establish piece rates (c)

visitas dirigidas (en turismo): guided tours (a)

vista aérea: a bird's eye view; aerial view (a)

voluntad férrea: ironclad will (a)

voluntad hidráulica: water saving policy; movement to economize on our use of waters (a,c)

voluntariedad: on a voluntary basis (b)

vuelta ciclística a Cuba: Cuban cross-country cycling race, cycling tour of Cuba (a)

Y

yacimiento (de petróleo): oil deposit (c)

Yate Gramma: GRANMA Cabin Cruiser (b)

Z

zafarrancho de combate: clearing for battle (b)

zafra: (c)

a) azucarera: sugarcane harvest

b) cafetalera: coffee harvest

c) citrícola: citrus harvest

d) de los Diez Millones: ten million-ton sugar harvest

e) del pueblo: People's cane harvest

f) socialista: socialist sugarcane harvest

zona:

a) afectada: (en el agua o la electricidad): problem zone (a)

b) cañera: sugarcane area (c)

c) congelada: reserved residential areas; exclusive residential areas (a)

d) de defensa: defense zone (b)

e) de desarrollo ganadero: cattle-raising area (c)

f) industrial: industrial area (c)

zoonosis: dog pound (a,c)

ACNOWLEDGEMENTS

Our unbounded affection to Professor and Translator **MARY TODD HAESSLER**, who has for years advised the author on this subject. Her patience, talent, experience, and assistance, always rendered with painstaiking kindness is highly valued.

Priceless and invaluable encouragement, advice and critical help from Professor **DOLORES MARIA CORONA**.

Sympathetic management in the organization and classification of the terms was provided by Professor **MIGDALIA ARAGONESES JEREZ.**

It fell to Professor **ESTEBAN PEREZ FERNANDEZ,** for the huge amount of editorial work that had to be done by our editor-in-chief, whom it was a real pleasure to work with.

We're forever indebted for wise counsel concerning general problems relating to the content format and arrangement of definitions as well as for expert judgement concerning many details to Professor **MARIA JOSEFA GOMEZ.**

Heartfelt thanks are due to, **ESTHER TATO, CARLOS LOPEZ, JANE Mc.MANUS and RENE DIAZ**, for having provided insights, suggestions and revision in this material.

We're much obliged to **DINORAH GRANDA CORTADA** for the selflessness and time devoted to the composition of this work

My heartfelt thanks and everlasting gratitude to Professor **MARJORIE MOORE REYNOLDS**, Ph.D. for the prologue in this book.and support throughout all these years of my career.and to all those who encouraged me to develop this glossary.

Another blue ocean press title

by Jesús Núñez Romay

Coming in Late 2007

Oddities in English by Jesús Núñez Romay
ISBN: 978-4-902837-05-6

One of the reasons why English can be such a hard language to learn is because of its many oddities- its many exceptions to rules and its varied phonetic pronunciations. This book gives the reader the tools to make sense these "oddities of the English Language" and become fluent speakers of the language in doing so.

blue ocean press

presents two new special book series:

1898 Consciousness Studies Series

'The Club of 1898' Consciousness Studies – The Club of 1898 are areas affected by the 1898 Treaty of Paris that granted possession of Spanish colonies to the United States - The Philippine Islands, Guahan (Guam), Puerto Rico, and Cuba.

The Spiritual Traveler Series

"The Spiritual Traveler Series provides the reader with a new type of travel writing experience. Instead of simply looking at the sights, sounds, and tastes of a locale, the Spiritual Traveler allows the reader to experience the consciousness of a nation".

"A Tourist takes in the local sights; a Traveler sees the reality of a landscape."

From the 1898 Consciousness Studies Series
and
The Spiritual Traveler Series

Cuba Is a State of Mind (The Spiritual Traveler Vol. I)
by p.w. long with Juaquin Santiago and Elijo Truth

Category: Travel - Sociology, Cultural Studies, Political Science, Current Affairs, Spirituality
Edition: First; Specifications: Softcover, 6 x 9, 80 pages; (2006)
Price: $12.95; ISBN: 978-4-902837-18-8

In writing on travel to Cuba, the Spiritual Traveler decides to give a voice to the Cuban Silent Majority.

The Silent Majority in Cuba are:
- Voices unheard in books about Cuba. We read about those who leave, but not about those who stay;   _
- Mostly black, mulatto, and rural white;
- Descendants of slaves;
- Masses of uneducated servants and peasant class before the Revolution. Those whose freedom was denied after their participation in the struggle during the Cuban War for Independence (1898);
- Loyal to Fidel;
- Most protective of the Revolution and subsequent Post-Revolutionary way of life so imbibed in African culture;
- Most affected by the US Blockade and least likely to receive remittances from relatives in the US;
- Those who would lose the most with a return to the Pre-Revolutionary status quo.

This is the first book to give voice to the Cuban Silent Majority, to hear their stories and know their consciousness. It gives future travelers to Cuba another perspective of Cuba to consider.

From the 1898 Consciousness Studies Series

Just Left of the Setting Sun by Julian Aguon

Category: <u>Essays</u> – Asia Pacific Studies, Political Science, Sociology, Women's Studies
Edition: First; Specifications: Softcover, 6 x 9, 88 pages; (2006)
Price: $13.95; ISBN: 978-4-902837-32-3

Just Left of the Setting Sun is a collection of non-fiction essays by a young Chamoru scholar-activist from the island of Guam. These essays reflect the present-day reality of the indigenous people of the island of Guam.

This book is framed in the context of an island that exists amidst the many conflicts and contradictions of being "freed from colonialism" by another colonial power in 1898 and "liberated from wartime aggression" by a country that put in under a Naval Administration until the 1960s and who worked to eliminate the culture of the local people through forced assimilation and nominal citizenship.

This book is written to articulate the reality of the Chamoru people of Guam as an indigenous Pacific Island culture, an American minority group, and an island people threatened by the encroachment of globalization into their lives. These essays will cause the reader to think critically on the subjects of globalization, sustainable development, sustainable governance, cultural reclamation, and self-determination on Guam, amongst the indigenous and colonized peoples in the world, question the value of democracy if it is involuntarily imposed on a people. This book is especially relevant for the present state of the world.

Just Left of the Setting Sun is included in an academic series that we publish, 'The 1898 Consciousness Studies Series'. This series is a varied collection of essays on consciousness today in areas affected by the Spanish-American War and consequent possession by the United States. These include The Philippines, Guam, Puerto Rico, and the Cuba.

To Order

blue ocean press books

For Individual Orders:

You can purchase and order blue ocean press books from your local bookstore; and you can find them on online retail sites such as:

http://www.amazon.com

http://www.powells.com

http://www.barnesandnobles.com

http://www.abebooks.com

For Institutional Buyers, Booksellers, and Libraries:

Books can be acquired from the following distributors/wholesalers:

Ingram/ ipage: (Toll Free) 1(800)937-0152, 1(615)793-5000

Ingram Library Services Inc.: (Toll Free) 1 (800)937-5300

Ingram International: 1(615)793-5000, (Canada T.Free) (800)289-0687

Ingram Book Group Website: http://www.ingrambookgroup.com

(In the UK)

Gardners Books Ltd.: 44(0)1323 521555 , (01323) 521777

Additional Ordering Questions:

For any questions on ordering books, please contact us at:

mail@aoishima-research.com or mail@blueoceanpublishing.com

CPSIA information can be obtained at www.ICGtesting.com

224168LV00002B/237/A